Third Eye Awakening

The Ultimate Guide on How to Open Your Third Eye Chakra to Experience Higher Consciousness and a State of Enlightenment

Paul Kain

Table of Contents

Introduction

I want to thank you and congratulate you for supporting this book, "Third Eye Awakening: The Ultimate Guide on How to Open Your Third Eye Chakra to Experience Higher Consciousness and a State of Enlightenment."

This book contains proven techniques and philosophies on how to become enlightened through the opening or waking of your third eye. The third eye is also known as the Anja chakra, the sixth chakra, the seat of the soul, and many other names. Most of us live day to day without knowing the amazing powers that come along with opening this eye.

Here's an inescapable fact: you want to develop your mental abilities to the fullest. Yet, undoubtedly there are blockages and fear that are preventing you from doing so.

If you do not foster your abilities, you are missing out on a gift that is innately within each and every one of us.

It's time for you to become more connected to the universe, basic truths, and your inner guidance and wisdom. You must learn how to open this third eye in order to live your life to the fullest and as an enlightened being.

Chapter 1:
What is the Third Eye?

Definition and History of the Discovery of the Third Eye

In Sanskrit *chakra*, or what we know as *chakra* literally means the "wheel" or the "ring." In regards to energy bodies, pathways for spirituality and health, there are actually many chakras throughout the body. They are considered nodes or energy points for the subtle body, that aspect of the human body that is not physical. They are the meeting points for energy channels that flow throughout the body in what would look like a magnetic field.

Ancient Hindu scriptures provide beautiful illustrations as to what chakras were known to look like, as well as their locations within the human body. They have not changed in our modern times. In fact, many cultures have adopted the chakra system into health, healing and spirituality practices. The body has seven main chakras of which we will be addressing the one, the sixth of the chakras, in depth within this book. Each of the chakras also involve specific colors, foods, crystals, their effect on the body, a history of their development for the individual, and also their inherent abilities.

The sixth chakra is called by a few names, which you will read here. One term is the *Aagya or Anja Chakra* which is the seat of the mysterious "third eye." Ajna means "command" (or also perceive), and it is related with knowledge, wisdom and intuitive powers. This energy point, or vortex, is seated between the eyebrows, just above the eyes, and centered in the forehead.

It is no doubt that you have seen images of a third eye on Hindu or Buddhist art, sculptures, television, on clothing or car bumper stickers. It is fascinating and for centuries has been viewed as sacred and special. The Third Eye, once opened, is also known as the Middle Eye of Shiva, a Hindu deity. In ancient Egyptian it was the Eye of Horus, which is image that lasts to this day.

Kundalini (the energy field) that carries the prana (energy), which travels from the first Chakra (at the base of the spine) to the seventh chakra or the crown at the top of the head. The sixth chakra is on the way to awakening this energy. It is also the seat of the Third Eye. Hindus also will place a red dot on the face at the point of the sixth chakra, to represent its abilities.

Another term for the sixth chakra is the Horn of the Unicorn. When the three high chakras prior are open as the kundalini energy rises, it moves upwards as a spiral into the crown chakra. The pointed spiral is in the likeness of a unicorn horn.

As we will see, along with centuries of wisdom and ancient practices, biochemically, there also is a scientific basis in western medicine. As there are endocrine glands and organs throughout the body that are involved in these processes as well, we will learn within the tantric teachings that the pituitary (in the sixth chakra) and the pineal (in seventh chakra) glands work on awakening the eye.

The teachings of the third eye tell us that is can be developed or awakened with practice and care. It can be stimulated to act in its most ideal form to provide insight, intuition, and a clarity of vision as well as to reveal the truth. It is responsible for a higher form of human consciousness.

The third eye chakra symbol has two elements that are associated with wisdom. The upside down triangle and the lotus flower, which is sometimes as a symbol, and sometimes pictorial. The lotus flower has two petals and usually is presented to be a white lotus, but the sixth chakra is associated with indigo or violet colors so it also may be illustrated with these colors.

The two petals, are supposed to portray nadis or the energy channels, which meet centrally before moving up into to the body's seventh chakra. They also represent the pineal and pituitary glands. The role of these endocrine glands will be discussed a bit later.

There is also Hindu deity that represents this chakra who is the part male and also female Shiva God and Shakti Goddess (named Hakini). In Sanskrit "ham" and "ksham" are on the petals written to represent each deity.

The balance of the two here is somewhat similar to the Yin and Yang. The half male and female deity ultimately represents this ultimate balance of the duality in people. The symbols used to represent the sixth or ajna chakra represent this.

Relationship between First and Second Eyes

The first and second eyes add to intuition, insight and the past and future that is a part of the abilities of the third eye or anja chakra. The first eye is one's physical sight and the second eye is representative of thought.

Opening the third eye is evolving the consciousness and an immense inner change of thought and being. Surprisingly to some, even in some philosophies the third eye is also about mystical thinking. Some liken it to *Christ consciousness*. The third eye transcends religions and philosophies but agree upon the integration and the growth of the conscious mind and deepest parts of the human spririt with the awakening of this capability in all human beings.

Uniqueness of the Third Eye

It is also said that the Third Eye is part of a higher dimension. Some refer to it as a conductor in the third dimension where humans exist. Energies and vibrations are received through the eye and allows the third eye taps into the higher senses, which we will explore more in this book. We will discuss the extensive history of its existence and powers, ranging from multi dimensions and all of the other five senses and deep insights. The third eye exists in a fourth dimension. With the open third eye, we can access these senses.

Since eyes process the light that is sensed and received, they usually need a lens through which to do this. As do human eyes, so does the Third Eye. The third eye is considered not of the physical body. It is also referred to as etheric or subtle. The etheric body overlays like a curtain with an energetic life force over your and is an invisible veil undetectable to most human eyes.

However, some can see the auras and this etheric body, in colors that symbolize the health and vitality of each area. Over the eye is a lens and through meditation the eye can be accessed.

Benefits of the Third Eye

When the sixth chakra, and the third eye, is balanced, there will be an inner guidance, which is a result of deep intuition and higher consciousness. It brings about a deeper spiritual knowledge that goes beyond intelligence. It allows for one to think, take action, or make decisions based upon innate truth and not obstructed views that are affected by superficiality or mistruths of the outer world and society.

This spiritual awakening joins the heart, mind and body, in that it aligns the chakras as the essential force moved upwards through the chakras. As long as these are balanced and open, the third eye will be able to open and the energy will also contribute to a lead to a higher consciousness. The awakening of the third eye is essential to human spiritual evolution.

Not everyone on the planet will chose to nor try to activate the third eye but we have the potentiality to do so if we want to put the effort and attention towards doing so. The benefits of opening this eye are immense. Having the eye allows us to tap into these natural and hidden gifts. As we further explore how to open this third eye, we will delve deeper into its gifts.

It provides emotional, physical and spiritual balance, as well as to see truth and deeper connections to thoughts and to people and things in our lives. We will feel more aligned with our higher purpose in life. It will minimize fears, and remove mental and emotional blockages. It will assist with activities such as decision making, intuitive guidance, bettering memory and abstract thought. We need these on a daily basis. We will experience better health, particularly in certain areas, and experience an abundance and fullness that we otherwise most likely would not have.

Interesting Facts about the Third Eye

Biologically, the third eye chakra is where the pituitary gland is but it is more often associated with the nearby pineal gland by some schools of philosophy regarding the third-eye. There are variations of the interpretation and purpose, as well as what is involved and what is more prominent however amongst the different schools of thought and faith.

The pituitary gland also has a spiritual significance which is also somewhat shared with the scientific role it has according to western medicine. Ancient cultures had knowledge and insight that far transcends modern text books. It is interesting where these two worldviews coincide.

The pituitary gland, in relation to spirituality and ancient cultures, has also been called the "seat of the mind." The pineal gland is also known as the "seat of illumination, intuition and cosmic consciousness". The pineal gland relates to the pituitary gland as the combining of functions to produce both intuition and reason. The glands join at an opening in the brain. Vibrations awaken the third eye. This can be done through sound and chanting.

According to one theory, we all had a true third eye on the back of each of our heads and that we evolved to a point where this eye shriveled and became our pineal gland. It allegedly has spiritual and physical functions, but no longer served as an external lens.

The true pineal gland also produces melatonin, the hormone that regulates our internal, circadian rhythms or cycles, such as our internal clocks that wake us up and that also make us tired. The pineal gland is also the gland where psychedelic DMT (the chemical, dimethyltryptamine) is made. The DMT is released at birth and death it is said. Some also say that there is a connection between the awakening of the third eye and the release of DMT from the pineal gland.

DMT is the only hallucinogen that is naturally occurring in the human body. Exactly when and how it is released is unknown and is and has been of study to science. It is believed that there is a role between the pineal gland, somehow tapping into and releasing the DMT and the awakening of the third eye, which leads one to obtain these other abilities and powers.

The tiny pituitary gland is between our eyes, and centered in the forehead, at the sixth chakra. The pineal gland is above the pituitary gland. It is pine-coned shaped. It is said that the joining of the essences of these two glands in the third ventricle is what opens the Third Eye. The two are responsible for intuition and thoughts in tandem.

You will see much imagery of pine cones, and thus the pineal (this pine-cone like) gland, in many places where the third eye, spiritual awakening, intuition and high spiritual knowledge is symbolized. Sometimes these top pillars, statues, appear in paintings or logos. This imagery is also across many religions and spiritual communities. Now that you are aware of part of its significance, you will most likely pay more attention to where you see these images and art forms and see them more often.

The pituitary gland, in sum, works to send messages to other glands to regulate some aspects of body growth and development. The pineal gland contains color sensory abilities like the human eyes. It also has a visual connections. This partially illustrates for you, the gland's role of receiving and communicating what happens with light and hormones in determining our circadian cycles.

The two glands are also working together on other purposes. The pineal gland also regulates some functions of the pituitary gland. First, the pituitary gland is responsible for triggering adolescence, including development, and puberty. The pineal gland keeps the pituitary from starting too early. Since it keeps the pituitary in check, it can be seen as curbing its impulses and puts a temporary hold on what it is meant to do.

Given how these two body structures communicate with each other, they seem to be able to trigger or pause human functions, and not only endocrine processes, but also to slow down or pause thinking. From a spiritual framework, the pause allows for time for what is meditation, and deep thinking.

It seems there is a connection between the purely medical interpretation of pineal and pituitary roles, and a significant role that the two play in raising human consciousness, but by using the same mechanisms. We do not know how ancient cultures knew this, but it is very complimentary way to look at human development if you consider the human being to be a spiritual one, merely living in a material world.

Another very interesting correlation to the third eye in humans is the connection to the parietal eye which is in some animals. It is a part of the epithalamus structure and associated with the pineal gland in these animals. The pineal gland is part of the structure, and the other half is the parietal eye with its own lens and retina (if fully developed in some species, whereas in others it may not be).These animals include some types of lizards, frogs, sharks, fish, and eels as a few examples.

The eye is has sensory abilities using different structures than the human eye, but structures that work in the similar way to receive and process light. In animals with this parietal eye, they also have hormonal communications systems as do humans, and similarly, these animal's circadian rhythms are also controlled through these photoreceptors. In mammals, this parietal organ is not there, but the pineal gland is, and carries some of the associated functions as when the two are present.

Myths about the Third Eye

One of the primary myths, or disbeliefs, about the third eye is that it is a myth! To date, we cannot diagnostically examine a skull and see a third eye, nor the chakra, nor the lens and the aura of the actual flesh and bone skull (although the latter is debatable, which we will make mere mention of later).

There are actually mythological stories about the purpose and development of the third eye. We will tell of one later. Historically in ancient Indian Tantric readings, and in Greek, Druid, and other cultural stories and myths, the role of the "Seer" is the one that accesses these third eye powers. They may also be presented as oracles, prophets, diviners, shamans, and sometimes magicians, or even witches.

You will see the eye, a cyclops-like one (in a Third eye position) and an all-seeing eye. Sometimes this person is characterized solely as a fortune teller, but in eastern traditions it is known that one who has the third eye awakened has all-encompassing possibilities. You will not sprout an eye but you will become more enlightened and intuitive once this has awakened.

Chapter 2:
Nine attainable psychic abilities

The third eye is the area responsible for the following psychic abilities. A bit will be described about each, below. By opening the third eye, one has the potential to access these abilities, which are inherent in all of us. However, most people do not try to tap into these abilities, or they may want to but they do not know how. This is where opening or awakening the third eye is important. This is the epicenter of these abilities.

It has been said that babies not only are born into this world as innocents but that they are born with the ability to see past the third dimension that most adults see and live in exclusively. It is assumed that we lose this ability as we adapt to our environment.

Each of these abilities is in fact unique, but you will see that they share qualities of extending the person past the three dimensional world and into at the very least a fourth dimensional world (or beyond). A person with any of these abilities is using their abilities of mind a spirit to tap into these other dimensional realms. Persons may on, some, or all of these abilities in combination or alone.

E.S.P. - Extra Sensory Projection, or ESP, encompasses anything beyond the five senses. It can be referred to as the sixth sense. It also can include a combination of many abilities of the below.

Telepathy - This ability involves being able to pick up on thoughts as a form of unspoken communication. It would be considered min-to-mind connection. Most commonly described as one-way as read by the one who has this ability, but sometimes can be two-way communication. This can be applied to humans as well as animals.

Clairaudience - This ability involves discerning sounds and voices that represent those not in these three dimensions. Clairaudients will say they hear a voice or a song of a dearly departed one, or of an ascended master. These can be clear sounds or symbolic or other representations.

Clairvoyance - This ability is different from the above, as it involves vision. Clairvoyants have the ability to see in the future, and sometimes in the past, future, or present. They are the ones often turned to find out what will be in someone's future, or what happened to someone in the past. This can be tangible or symbolic as well.

Clairsentience - This ability is also different as it has to do with feeling. A clairsentient person has the ability to pick up on feelings that provide information, either that is clear or that may be symbolic to the clairsentient.

Channeling - This involves usually involves a person (the channel) allowing their body and mind to by a conduit or channel for messages or healing. Sometimes it is quite conversational and other times there will be a trance like state of the channel. The person channeling is reaching out and drawing in the energy, sometimes of a messenger, or of a person who has passed on, an ascended master, or a deity, and communicating with them through the channel.

The channel will sometimes speak in their own voice, or speak in the voice of or just directly from the person or entity being channeled. Additionally, they may or may not recall what was said. It also involves interpretation, or translation (literal or metaphorical), and sometimes the use of the above abilities as well.

Automatic Writing - This is similar to channeling above, but the person who has this ability will be able to enter into a state that will channel automatic messages that provoke the person to begin writing messages that are received in this way. They may be matter of fact writings, or they may need some interpretation as well.

Mediumship - A medium is similar to channeling except the medium makes that connection in a usual state, to make contact with a deceased person or animal usually on behalf of someone who wishes to have that contact or ask information of the deceased individual. Sometimes it is used to discover unknown information or to get closure for the living.

Astral Projection - This involves being able to enter a lucid-dream like state in between a wakeful state and falling into a deep sleep. Upon reaching this state, the person will be able to project themselves into another dimension called the astral plane, where location is universal and boundless. The person may project their light being to any location, no matter how far. The person can recollect this projection once they return to their physical bodies.

Each of these abilities has unique ways of being developed, and some can be developed in unison. Each brings special gifts to the person who has the ability to use their third eye, the sixth or Anja chakra, to tap into these powers for helping reveal truth to the person, and also for the bettering of humanity.

Chapter 3:
Awakening the Third Eye

Why should you open or awaken the Third Eye?

In various religions or spiritual communities there are techniques and practices involving the development and the awakening of the third eye. Sometimes the goal is merely to understand the person's current reality as it is, and others may have the diverse and deeper spiritual goals as discussed.

The benefits to opening the third eye in terms of personal development, higher spiritual attainment and a deeper connectedness to the world in and around us are discussed in prior chapters. The chapter prior also addressed the expansion of psychic abilities which adds another layer to the potentiality of awakening and opening this third eye. Opening this "divine eye" is essentially clearing one's vision in the ways applicable to the use and the multiple gifts of the third eye.

Activating and cleaning the Third Eye can bring clarity, intuition, concentration, new perspective, and insight as well as some of the following other attributes and abilities.

• Creativity and imagination are expanded.

• Seeing and/or feeling energy, auras, fields, and possibly the ability to conduct energy healing.

- Visions of other dimensional worlds and beings or thought forms. At times, even hearing sounds from the fourth dimension

- Deeper sleeping, and more vivid and often, the ability to have lucid dreams.

- Astral projection may be possible.

According to Hinduism, many negative qualities such as indecisiveness, uncertainty, envy, negativity, and confusion may come from having a closed third eye.

Experiences upon Awakening the Third Eye

Some who feel and sense that their third eye has opened will see imagery, or see or sense other worldly beings. They also report to have instant or gradual increases in psychic abilities. Some report better health and better sleep. They explain a better connectedness with others, nature and themselves. Many report to see and feel universal truths that transcend book knowledge, and go beyond superficial worldliness. We discuss the possibilities within this book. Those who have intentionally opened this eye do so for these reasons and they are amazed when it is revealed to them.

These can be strange and frightening to some. Many will learn to develop and work with these, and some may close themselves off. It is unknown territory within the power of our minds. It also may be difficult to feel for the first time that the seer of everything in your life is through a lens that is spiritual and not the scientifically described mechanisms we are all taught in grade school.

Purifying and Awakening the Third Eye

Through poor diet, exposure to toxins, stress and modern lifestyle choices, it has been thought that the pineal gland becomes hardened, calcified and shuts down. We will explain here some methods to detoxify your pineal gland and activate it, so you can reach a whole new perception and understanding of Reality.

To prepare yourself for activating the third eye you must control your environment, both internal and externally, your body, and your spiritual mind.

First we will focus on the physical body. What we ingest has a strong relationship to our ability to progress spiritually. Particularly as we prepare for the opening of the third eye, we want to maintain a clarity of vision and body function to move us forward in our journey. If there are blockages, the journey will be more difficult and present special challenges.

The pineal gland is said to be atrophied, shriveled, and not working to its fullest potential in most persons in modern society due to diet and environment as well as mental and spiritual non-use. To begin, we should start the process of detoxification.

The grouping of the chemicals that we are first concerned with fall under a group called halides. These also include fluorides, bromides and chlorines. Fluorides where exist in our water supply in most parts of the western world. They also exist in our foods that are grown or prepared in fluoridated water, and they are in our toothpastes and mouth washes. We swim and bathe in them.

The fluoride is a main culprit in the calcification of the pineal gland, as it will accumulate in the brain and in the pineal gland specifically. It takes effort to eliminate these chemicals from our lives, but it takes attention and work to change our eating, drinking and bathing or swimming habits. Yet it should be changed and these chemicals should be avoided if you wish to detoxify and cleanse the pineal gland. Meditation and other practices alone will be helpful, but if the gland itself cannot function because it has calcified and weakened, it will be extremely difficult to do much to awaken the third eye.

There are quite a few ways to make changes that you can research that may include how to switch your drinking water, ways to filter your drinking and your bathing water, how to avoid chlorinated pools, and to limit the other ways that your body is exposed to these three harmful chemicals.

Mercury is another element that should be avoided. Dental fillings also can be removed and changed if this is an option.

Calcium takes many forms. The most common type that we are exposed to is the dietary calcium. Any calcium that ingested above and beyond our regular, natural whole food intake is excessive and the body will store it.

Ironically, it will be leached from where we need it the most. This affects the ability to calcify bones but also the calcification of organs that we do not want to be calcified (such as the pineal gland). In the western world we have the most dairy consumption but also the highest rates of bone loss and arthritis. If this is what happens to legs and wrists, imagine what the tiny, extremely sensitive and important feature called the pineal gland?

We will address foods that should be eaten and supplements that should be ingested later, but here we will mention at the least that foods grown in or having pesticides applied later, are also toxic to the pineal gland.

Other purification techniques may include using crystals and magnets. A more comprehensive explanation of crystals and the use of them in awakening the third eye will follow. A magnet can also be used to cleanse the third eye, by removing calcification. You can try by placing an adhesive magnet to where the third eye is located. Do this a few times throughout the day to stimulate the pineal gland. This exercise can be used to decalcify the pineal gland. It also simulates the earth's geomagnetic field properties and its affects upon stimulating the pineal gland as well.

Other activities which are also techniques for awakening the third eye can be done also in preparation, as well as for maintaining the third eye awareness for as long as you would like. These include:

- Yoga

- Meditation

- Chanting

Other factors involved in opening the third eye have to do with one's environment. You should practice preparation as well as any awakening activities within a calm and relaxing environment. You also would not want any interruptions, so be sure that you will not be disturbed or your concentration and mental clarity will be disrupted.

Remove electronics from your sight and contact. If you can be in a room completely free of electronics this is much better. These devices emit blue light which impacts your melatonin and serotonin (a pleasure and relaxation chemical) levels and affects the pineal gland. They also produce electromagnetic frequencies, which are also disruptive.

Close windows, curtains, blinds and doors to create partial darkness. If you can be in total darkness for some activities this is also very helpful. If there is very slight light you may be able to start to process people's auras. Some may also begin to see other energy and spiritual beings. Some may see these things in total darkness.

Stimulating the pineal gland helps to prepare its awakening and also to decalcify it. Picture a tree shaking in the wind to release snow that weighs down its branches. Visualize the pineal gland being gently shaken to release its own binds.

Breathing clean air is also important, either by being in nature, or an enclosed screened area when it is dark. You may also purify your home air with filters.

Techniques

These techniques are some of the more common that you will find to promote the opening of the third eye, or ajna chakra. They are simple ways to help to change the focus from our third dimensional selves from the outer world to the higher spheres of being. This allows us to be receptive to working with and awakening the third eye. Now that we are preparing to do the work, we must remind ourselves of our purpose.

The Trataka Technique- This is a meditation technique used to create awareness of the third eye, and to awaken it. It is a third eye meditation based on the kundalini energy that we have discussed earlier. The instant state of meditation involves around this sixth center of consciousness, and stimulating this in a physical and spiritual sense. We have discussed the flow of the prana or energy and how it moves upwards, through the seven chakras as kundalini energy. In the path of the Kundalini is the sixth chakra. In this Trataka, or sixth chakra meditation, will we use to focus on the third eye.

The make-up of the third eye lens, and where it is positioned spiritually is partially why we can develop the perception with our inner eye. The third eye lens' point in our aura is the focal point while meditating. This technique also puts the brain into a deep consciousness happens in meditation, and in sleep, in vivid images in the quasi awake states before and after sleeping and awaking. This exercise also helps develop intuition and inner guidance.

To do this properly, you should close your eyes and be seated comfortably and upright. If you are able it is better to sit in what is known as the lotus pose, upright and cross-legged.

While breathing start to let your eyes relax and while your eyes are still closed, turn them upward so that you are looking at your own third-eye from the inside. To focus and keep this position, try counting backwards from one hundred. Do this while you are breathing slowly and deeply in and out, for at least five breaths.

When you are done you may stretch it to simply observing and allowing thoughts to pass through your mind and eye. Still focus on the eye as well as your breathing. You will feel an energy flowing upward with each breath that you take. Do this for fifteen minutes.

You also will find that your eyes may strangely feel still, relaxed, and that you are probably able to maintain this position effortlessly as well. Make sure your breaths are slow and gentle and that you are not holding them. You may feel still, calm, aware but relaxed, and your third eye area may feel warm. Some say that they see their thoughts, and feel that they now know where they came from and from where their eyes perceive what they see. After this time, while you are still breathing slow and steady, relax your eyes and mind with the intention that you are ready to let this meditation go. Let your attention move to your visual first eyes and let the focus leave from the third eye. Then open your eyes.

Yoga

Yoga brings brings all parts of a person together in many ways. Yoga reverses the the body's energy and brings it back inwards to help increase awareness.

Shiva yoga focuses on the pineal gland and wakes up the third eye. There are however, many types of yoga, and some have shared philosophies and postures. Below are a few of the hundreds of postures that are also very helpful in awakening the third eye. You should study these with a teacher for best results, but you can do research or watch videos and try them in combination with other parts from this book.

- Balasana or Child's pose

- Janu Sirsasana or Head-to-Knee Pose

- Makarasana or Dolphin pose

  Some of the more advanced yoga positions are:

- Garudasana or Eagle pose

- Handstand

- Yog Nidra

Essential Oils

These carry the essences of plants and herbs. Since they are from living things, they also have their vibrations and energy as well as contain many healing abilities. Their use for the third eye awakening are to stimulate the third eye, address any blockages, and to maintain the flow of energy. There are many that can be used, but a few of the most commonly used and available in many countries are below.

Bay Laurel essential oil facilitates and heightens psychic abilities. Stimulates brain (left-rational brain, right-creative brain) synchronization awareness.

Carrot Seed is said to heal eyesight, physically and spiritually, and allows for clarity of vision. It also balances the bodies, both etheric and physical, and can be used in this manner for third eye work.

Chamomile calms an help objectively examine thoughts and patterns and discern those that do not serve us.

Clary Sage also helps with sight and disorders of the brain, ranging from mild and severe.

Jasmine helps with deep pain and emotional issues. It also helps facilitate connection and intuition. Jasmine heightens bodily senses.

Melissa helps open fourth chakra, take you to higher realms and higher energy and activating the pineal.

Palo Santo helps aid purification and it grounds, facilitates spiritual awareness and enhances the ability to sense other realms.

Rose calms and relaxes. It is also symbolic of opening of the anja chakra. Ironically it has the highest vibrations of all of the essential oils, which sounds to be a contradiction.

With third eye awakening practice, we are relaxing and calming the mind but also accessing higher vibrational dimensions than the one we live in. It is actually quite fitting to have assistance from this calming and yet spiritually highly energetic oil.

Some others that are useful as well, and may compliment these primary and quintessential third eye chakra oils are below. You can do a bit of research and see which properties fit your needs and select some to start with. You should also learn how to properly use the oils and do not underestimate their abilities. Some can be applied, some are simply aromatic. Some may be toxic if ingested. Not all are made the same and they each have their own properties. Be sure to do some homework before you work with these very potent oils. They should be respected.

- Angelica Root

- Cypress

- Elemi

- Frankincense

- Helichrysum

- Juniper

- Marjoram

- Patchouli

- Rosemary

- Sandalwood

- Vetiver

Crystals

Some commonly used crystals for awakening the third eye are listed below. Other appropriate crystals may also be purple, violet or indigo or over into the blue range. As mentioned prior, the color that corresponds with the Anja chakra is a violet purple. Some very good crystals to use are:

- Amethyst

- Azurite Sun

- Blue Aventurine

- Blue Tourmaline

- Dumortierite

- Fluorite

- Lapis Lazuli

- Shungite

- Sugilite

- Quartz

The stones may be placed singly, together, in patterns, or worn on or around the body. Do some research on the crystals that feel intuitively of interest to you, and begin there. You can also go into a store that sells crystals and stones, and pick up and touch them to see which feel right. Sometimes the vibrational frequency of the crystal will feel different to you and you will be drawn to its energy.

Similar to the oils, each stone has its own properties. You can use your research to select the properties that you would like, and to learn about other crystals that you may want to find. Also, you can research the many things that you can do with crystals, where to place them, how to align them, how to clean them, and more. Wear them, sleep near them.

A simple technique to use to get you accustomed to using the crystals is to place them on your body while you are practicing meditation. Lay down and place one on the anja chakra area while you breathe slowly and calmly. You can combine this with meditation as well.

If you can do these a few times a day and they will help with the awakening. The different crystals have various properties. For instance, Amethyst increases intuition. Lapis lazuli facilitates connection and higher awareness. It is very good to practice this with a meditation.

There are some crystals that in addition to those listed above, have benefit to stimulate and cleanse the pineal gland. These include:

- Angelite

- Axinite

- Celestite

- Chiastolite

- Labradorite

- Laser Quartz

- Moonstone

- Phenacite

- Pietersite

- Rhodonite

- Sapphire (Purple)

- Tourmaline (Purple Violet)

- Sodalite

You can specifically target the pineal gland by using one of these particular crystals above, wither as a stone or as the tip of a crystal wand (which you can also purchase where you purchase most crystals).

This exercise can be done outside in the sun. The crystals collect and concentrate the sun's cosmic rays and channel them into the brow chakra. Do a simple meditation with a focus on the awareness of the third eye. Do this every day for about five to fifteen minutes or more.

Open Portal Technique

The third eye is a part of the Anja chakra as you now know. As we discussed, the lens for the third eye is part of the aura at the sixth chakra. This is the sixth energy point, or wheel, or ring as it is also referred as you move up from the root chakra. Chakras can also be considered to be vortexes of energy, as they rotate at each chakra point. In order to open the third eye by way of its lens, we must open the sixth chakra portal.

Starting in a dark area, sitting or lying comfortably and without interruption you may begin your meditation as we have described. As you focus on your third eye, you will visualize the lens opening and a portal between this three dimensional world and a fourth dimensional world being created. This portal would allow you the sight and vision that would be required to open your eyes. It also gives you the vision to open your deeper mind to the subtle bodies, thought forms, and energy and light beings that may be on this other side.

When doing this, you will be opening up your thoughts and sights to a new reality and vision of a different layer to the world.

Other techniques to opening the third eye:

Scrying

To practice the ancient technique known as scrying, you will be steadying your sight essentially by staring, and focusing in one place for a while, which will be a stone here for the use of the example. Some persons use mirrors on which to scry. Others will use still water, fire gaze, or use candles for similar purposes.

You will start by trying to relax and clear your mind. Close your eyes and then open them when you are ready, so that you can begin to look at the stone. As you gaze into the stone, you also will allow the object to blur or fade away if needed, in order to allow images to begin to appear on the scrying stone. You may get a vision on the stone. There are stones for this such as polished pink quartz (which is semi-translucent), and that you can purchase for scrying. The scrying stones will have a smooth or sometimes even a flat surface that you can use for this purpose.

Symbolism

As you meditate, scry, dream, and increasingly awaken the third eye, images will come through the lens and into your third eye. Some will be immediately recognizable and may be meaningful, while others will need interpretation or even more meditation. Trust your intuitive instincts on what these symbols mean to you, or feel like to you, etc. Keep note of the symbolism as you go. Research and purchase a good book on symbols, or use an online version. Any store that sells crystals and rocks usually carries books of this nature as well, or they can refer you to one.

Dreams

Dream imagery is some of the most exquisite of visions, and is usually rich in symbolism. Through dreams we gain access to communications, people, energy beings, places and more. Dream work affects waking life and likewise, work in the waking life related to the third eye reciprocally affects dreaming.

Sound

The use of sound is yet another way to awaken the third eye. Using another of the five senses, again, we are tapping into a sixth. Sound can be used in a few different ways in regards to opening this eye.

Chanting is a practice in and of itself and is not just about making noise. It serves a higher purpose. Chanting in meditation balances the spirit, mind, and body. It is also healing. In light of the third eye and our intention to open and awaken it, chanting can be used to make bones in the nasal area, to vibrate and awaken the pineal gland.

Bija Mantra or Seed Mantra

The Bija (seed) mantras are one syllable sounds that activate the chakras by speaking them, chanting them, and causing a reverberation as stated above. Om or Ohm, of "Pranava Om," is what is called a seed syllable, a basic sound of the universe that contains all other sounds. The sound "Om" which you may have heard as it is quintessentially a sound that is used in meditation and sometimes it is even incorporated in yoga practice. The Om sounds also reverberates within the sixth chakra and increases awareness, helping to open and awake the third eye. They are used to purify and balance the chakras and bring an awareness to the needs of that chakra area. For this purpose, we would especially like to balance the sixth chakra.

Sound Healing

Sounds can be used to balance and heal. In the case of the third eye, you will want to purify, cleanse the vision and increase the energy in this chakra. Chimes, singing bowls, tuning forks, and songs are also used for opening the third eye. Humming is another technique. The sound "Thoh" is also used to produce a resonation in the chakra area when chanted through the slightly opened mouth and using the tongue and the teeth. It would sound like the word "toe", and chanted in a lower but still natural voice.

Binaural beats are also amazing ways to activate the chakra. They are also used in general for healing and awareness techniques for a variety of purposes. Using binaural beats for activating the sixth chakra would invoke heightened consciousness with very specific sound frequencies. When selecting a binaural beat (which you can buy on a CD or just use some that you research online), you will see the purpose of the binaural beat along with the sound frequency usually stated in Hertz (Hz).

Another strategy is to sit yourself in a dark or semi-dark place, and gather a variety of percussion instruments such as bowls, chimes, triangles, or anything else you may have or be able to fashion yourself, and create your own sound that feels good and that resonates with you. You can do this at any time. It also make help you get comfortable with letting loose and being able to do some of the other activities and practices listed here, especially if they feel a bit strange at first.

How to tell that the Third Eye is Open

When the third eye opens, some say it is a gradual awakening, but many say it just happened when some threshold tipping point. Many say they had felt heat at the site of the third eye when attempting to awaken it, as well as a twitchy vibration, or throbbing or pulsating, about an inch beneath the skin on the forehead, and that it evolved from there. Some say it accompanied a headache or migraine at worst. This can also be said of the practices to awaken the third eye, but will ease with experience and practice.

Some experience a transformation in clarity and vision. Others have reported seeing the eye open from the eye within, and entities crossing through. Some others have seen colors and imagery that they knew was not due to their first eyes.

An interesting and often reported sign has been a popping or clicking sound and a shaky sensation that occurs at some point when practicing the awakening exercises. The exercises do take time however, and need to be part of a disciplined practice, not just a casual attempt now and then, to be most beneficial.

You may immediately experience a significantly heightened intuitive and probably other psychic abilities (including vision, hearing and feeling). You may also see energy beings and auras. These are some of the common signs that your third eye is awake and open.

Common Challenges to Awakening the Third Eye

There are many people that would think obtaining this mental clarity, intuition and the possibility of psychic powers would be an amazing feat but they may not know how, feel comfortable, or feel that it actually could be successful. Often time's people may fear not just the unknown but the thought that something may actually happen. Then they would need to figure out what to do!

Knowing what the techniques, philosophies and practices are surrounding the awakening of the third eye are daunting. That is one purpose of this book. This should not be daunting nor impossible. The opening of the third eye is something that all humans are born with the potential to do. Yet it is still a challenge in many spiritual, emotional and physical ways.

It takes concentration, focus and meditation. Many people in modern societies feel they already do not have time to exercise or meditate, never mind that our thoughts are always moving and seem to be incessant. We think too much when we sleep and have restless nights. The process of awakening the third eye requires intentional focus and concentration in order to calm and to clear the mind. This is difficult for many to do easily.

Some physical issues such as the development of strange, unknown experiences and sensations and headaches may keep some from attempting or continuing these practices. Some have also reported that they were not comfortable with certain abilities or events. For instance, some people have told of the psychic abilities that they were not aware of, and that they did not want to have as strongly. Others have been frightened by the opening of the vortex and visions of beings and entities crossing through at random, unpredictable times.

Opening the third eye does not have to be scary however, and much study can be done on how to ground and protect oneself (before, during, and after) using some of the materials and practices described in this book, and elsewhere. You can also find a teacher, master or guru who is reputable and experienced to assist you so you do not have to do these intense things on your own.

The awareness and abilities related to awakening the third eye are endless and although it may cause some emotional discomfort at some levels, we do not need to settle for what is immediately comfortable.

Closing the Third Eye

It is very helpful to know how to do this at the beginning but also at any time after the third eye has been opened. Too much energy may be coming through and you may not know yet what to do to slow it or to close it, or even how to open it back up at your desire. Having a process in place before you open the eye is important.

To close the third eye and its abilities for any given reason, we can suggest you do so in one of a few ways. The teacher, guru or master may be able to help you individually.

There are many visualizations and meditations that you could do at this time. Here is one recommended activity where you use your conscious and unconscious to view the third eye as a large lotus flower. Address any spirit guides or angels, positive entities, or ascended beings who have met you along the way, or who may have guided you at this time if you have them. If not, address the universe, or the God of your creation in thanking them for this gift but at this time you would like to either return it or put it to rest temporarily. Now put your focus and intentions on gently doing so.

- First ground yourself, and utilizing crystals or oils if you chose.

- Start by getting comfortable in the physical lotus (cross-legged) position, or by laying down, or another comfortable posture.

- Close your eyes and begin to breath slowly and deeply until you are relaxed.

- Begin by visualizing the flower petals opening and closing as you breathe, and watch them as they are getting smaller and smaller. These will represent your sixth chakra.

- Visualize the energy leaving the subtle body as returning to your body.

- Pull your aura back in closer to your physical body by visualization.

- Visualize a pink bubble around you, surrounded by white light. This bubble with protect you and keep you grounded, but not entirely closed off.

- State aloud that you are closing the lens at that moment and slowing or stopping all energy and senses that flow through that lens. Also state aloud that you may choose to open up later if you so wish.

- Watch the petals get smaller until they disappear into a tiny center which looks like a vortex that is closing and fading away.

- Finish with a message of gratitude and gently remove yourself from the meditation and open your eyes.

Another technique is to send kundalini energy in a reverse pattern through the seven chakras. You can do this on a daily basis to control the flow of energy. Do things of your daily life other than the spiritual realm and your third eye abilities that have awakened. This may sound counterintuitive for what you intended to do by opening up the eye, but it is wise and helpful to slow down and redirect this new energy if it is uncomfortable.

You can also use crystals, stones, other meditations and yoga to slow or stop the flow of the sixth chakra's energy. A simple Epsom salt, Celtic sea salt or Himalayan salt bath has also been recommended by psychics!

Chapter 4:
Psychic Abilities

How to Become a Psychic Medium

If you do want to keep your third eye open and develop your abilities you must also follow the words of advice in prior chapters. Do your homework to know what you are opening yourself up to, and how to do this properly. Get grounded. Use crystals, oils, meditation, chanting, yoga, etc. Find a teacher to instruct you and to mentor you. It would still be very valuable to know how to turn it on and off if you choose as well. If you wish to develop these gifts further, here are some activities you can practice.

Ten Ways to Develop your Psychic Abilities

You should committee to practicing one activity each day. Practice it so that it is natural and comfortable, and then add another and do the same.

1. Meditate

When you meditate daily, you are connecting to the universe and raising your vibration and consciousness. You must raise your own vibration to meet those of the spiritual world which is already at a very high vibrational level. Meditate for ten to fifteen minutes a day to start. Increase by five minutes as you can.

2. Psychometry

This is reading energies of things. Practice by holding something (something with history, or metal would contain a lot of energy). Try to relax and gather impressions to see or hear anything about it's past. You can also try to meditate upon it.

3. Clairvoyance-Flowers

This activity will involve developing one's clairvoyant abilities utilizing a flower visualization. Using fresh flowers placed in front of you, simply notice them for a few minutes and then close your eyes. With your eyes closed, picture each flower in your mind to develop the image. If you gather any perceptions from this as well that is even better! Develop the mental pictures as you go.

4. Clairvoyance- Random

This is similar to the prior activity but with randomness. Get comfortable and begin to place your mind on your third eye area. Try not to think, but let your mind bring images into your lens of the eye. Let them come and let them pass, noting them as they appear.

5. Antique Stores

These are great places to visit as they have so many histories, involving people and places that will reveal themselves to you if you develop your ability to get in tune with them. The antiques also carry their own vibrations. Note what you feel or hear or see when you do this. Do this anytime you are able to visit one and practice as much as possible, paying attention to how your senses develop.

6. Symbol Books

Our senses often pick up symbols that eventually need to be interpreted, they are not always at face value. While you are developing your abilities it is a great idea to keep track of the various symbols that you will interface with. Practice this while alone. In a quiet place or even a light meditative state ask spirit to show you symbols for things that you are thinking and note them in a book that you have for this purpose. You may find them come up in the future and these may be part of your interpretive vocabulary.

7. Clairaudience

To develop psychic hearing abilities. Pay more and closer attention to every day sounds in your environment to increase your awareness. You will learn to pay attention to sounds as you are picking up sounds now that your third eye is awakened.

8. Family Pictures

Gather some older family pictures. Go as far back as you possibly can. Use your ability to sense things through the energy in the photo that you possibly can. Note them as well. Try this with different pictures and expand to people you may not know for impressions.

9. Journal

Ask for guidance on something that may be an obstacle in your life and note what thoughts may come to you. These senses may come in other forms that you need to interpret, which may be another layer to noting them in writing. You should also keep a dream journal, and use it immediately (no more than 10 seconds after waking!), in order to recall some of the many dreams that you most likely had throughout the night.

10. Vibrational Foods

Eating healthy, whole, and organic, high vibration foods not only is better for your overall physical health but it is good for your psychic health as well. Similar to what was already said about meditation and raising your vibration, you can use food to raise your vibration. If you eat poor foods it will lower this. You need the higher energy vibrations to work in higher realms.

Do your research well. Living foods, especially raw and organic foods and organic produce that are free of things such as radiation, growth in farm sewage and other tainted waters, and pesticides, larvicides, fungicides, etc.

A special form of photography that was developed in Russia and Eastern Europe called Kirlian photography has shown that even our foods can have colored auras! These auras represent vital life forces or energy that radiate from the food. Raw and organic food has the largest energy fields. Examples of this may be raw broccoli or orange slices have higher fields than cooked and "dead" foods such as boiled broccoli or a steak have the lowest energy fields. Even raw fish versus cooked fish has shown a higher energy field.

Avoid processed foods, artificial foods that are presented as food (but are not), and foods with added chemicals. You should also avoid any stimulants including caffeine. Alcohol can be a nervous system stimulant as well as a nervous system depressant. Either function agitates the body. It is also toxic to the body and the mind. Any meats that are ingested should be as fresh as possible. If you eat energetic foods, you become what you eat, which is full of vibrational life forces.

In order to support your third eye awakening and development, you must do all that you can to increase and sustain your vibrational energy. We as humans in this three dimensional world have challenges, but we can learn to adjust and raise these vibrational energies by our lifestyles, through meditation, yoga and other exercise, through positive thinking and the other strategies in this book.

Conclusion

Thank you again for supporting this book!

I hope this book was able to help you to understand the role of your third eye and how to best develop and awaken it.

The next step is to work on some of these activities on your own, and let this book be your guide. You may explore your consciousness and evolve as a person by following some of the techniques here.

Finally, if you enjoyed this book, please take the time to share your thoughts and post a review on Amazon. It'd be greatly appreciated!

Thank you and good luck!

Description

This book explores the mysterious third eye. The third eye is also known as the sixth chakra of the seven main chakras. It is the energy point for developing intuition, inner powers, clear decision making, balancing the inner and outer worlds, and the evolution of one self.

By awakening the third eye one will tap into these powers as well as psychic abilities. These are true abilities to see beyond the constraints of this three dimensional world that we live in. You only must be open to this possibility as well as the abilities you will acquire to receive them.

In this book you will learn:

- The history of the third eye also known as the sixth chakra

- How the chakra relates to both to spirituality and science

- The psychic abilities that come with an open chakra

- Techniques for opening the third eye including meditation, crystals, and oils

- The effects and challenges of awakening the third eye

- How to maintain a higher vibrational life to keep this eye open

Made in the USA
Middletown, DE
03 February 2017